AF226710

THE ATTACHMENT DRAMA HEALING METHOD™

A Transformative Guide to Understanding Attachment Conflicts, Emotional Wounds, and Healing Patterns Across the Relationship Cycle

By

Johanna Sparrow
Antoinette M. Watkins

Blue Shoes Publishing

Dedication

Dedicated to the ones who loved through chaos, survived through silence, and healed through pain. To every heart that kept going when it didn't feel seen this is your return to yourself.

MISSION STATEMENT

THE ATTACHMENT DRAMA HEALING METHOD™

My mission is to help you overcome troubling attachment styles that interrupt your daily life, causing unhappiness through the cycles of fear, avoidance, conflict, and disconnection. You will heal through the Attachment Drama Healing Method™. Because we'll dive deep into the roots of your attachment style and how the injuries occurred while creating a practical, supportive pathway toward emotional safety and healing.

The Johanna Sparrow method blends storytelling, symbolic pattern recognition, self-reflection, and behavior awareness to illuminate how attachment styles appear in genuine relationships. It is designed to meet readers, partners, families, and individuals wherever they are offering tools that reveal not only what is happening between people but also what is happening within them.

My mission is to help you understand your emotional language, claim your healing, and break the cycles that have followed you for years so your relationships can flourish. This method is more than a framework it is a guide, a mirror, and a bridge toward healthier connections that flourish a lifetime.

May this book serve as your foundation for healing, emotional regulation, and relationship transformation.

Johanna Sparrow
Creator of the Attachment Drama Healing Method™Page 5
Blue Shoes Publishing

Attachment Drama Healing Method™ Symbol System Overview

The Attachment Drama Healing Method™ uses a set of intuitive visual symbols to help readers quickly recognize emotional patterns, attachment responses, and relational dynamics as they appear throughout this book.

These symbols act as **anchors** reminders of recurring emotional themes that influence how we love, protect ourselves, and relate to others. When you see these icons within the reflection sections, chapter headings, or exercise prompts, they are guiding you toward a deeper layer of insight.

Each symbol represents a specific attachment pattern or emotional state you could identify with as it relates to your attachment style:

- ■ **Secure Attachment — The Square**
- Stability, groundedness, emotional availability
- ▲ **Avoidant Attachment — The Triangle**
- Independence, withdrawal, self-protection
- ● **Anxious Attachment — The Circle**
- Pursuit, emotional looping, closeness-seeking
- ◑ **Fearful-Avoidant — The Split Circle**
- Push–pull, ambivalence, mixed signals
- △ **Commitment Phobia — The Hollow Triangle**
- Presence without depth, fear of intimacy

- ♉ **Narcissistic Cycles — The Spiral**
- Idealize–discard patterns, emotional turbulence
- ◎ **Codependency — The Linked Rings**
- Enmeshment, blurred boundaries, over-functioning
- ▮ **Stonewalling — The Block**
- Emotional cutoff, shutdown, disconnection
- ⚡ **Emotional Chaos — The Lightning Line**
- Reactivity, dysregulation, unpredictable responses
- 🌱 **Healing — The Seedling**
- Growth, restoration, emotional maturation
- ◉ **Secure Future Self — Integrated Stability**
- Wholeness, clarity, emotional regulation

These symbols appear throughout the book to help you visually track your emotional landscape, recognize repeating behaviors, and understand the attachment dynamics influencing your relationships.

Use them as touchpoints on your healing journey they are designed to support clarity, empowerment, and overall healing.

TABLE OF CONTENTS

Introduction

CHAPTER 3 — The Drama Cycle™

- Trigger » Reaction » Collapse » Reconnection
- Why People Repeat Painful Patterns
- Attachment-Based Conflict Loops
- Reflection & Integration

CHAPTER 4 — Emotional Trauma in Relationships

- Breakups
- Divorce
- Betrayal
- Loss
- Abuse
- Neglect
- Abandonment Wounds
- Reflection & Integration

CHAPTER 5 — Communication From Each Attachment Style

- How Each Style Fights
- How Each Style Loves
- Shutdowns, Pursuits & Emotional Flooding
- Reflection & Integration

CHAPTER 6 — The Attachment Drama Healing Method™ Framework

- Step 1: Identification
- Step 2: Regulation
- Step 3: Core Wound Work
- Step 4: Emotional Reparenting

CHAPTER 7 — Healing Yourself

- Journaling
- Boundaries
- Emotional Regulation
- Somatic Awareness
- Nervous System Safety
- Reflection & Integration

CHAPTER 8 — Healing Relationships

- Dating
- Marriage
- Family dynamics
- Parenting
- Co-parenting
- Reconciling after emotional injury
- Reflection & Integration

CHAPTER 9 — When Healing Isn't Enough

- Recognizing Patterns That Cannot Change
- Walking Away with Clarity
- Rebuilding After Loss
- Reflection & Integration

CHAPTER 10 — Becoming Secure

- The Path to Emotional Maturity
- The New Relationship Model
- What Future Generations Need
- Final Reflection & Next Steps

INTRODUCTION

Understanding the Emotional Patterns That Shape Your Life

Most individuals carry heartbreaking and emotional wounds they can feel but cannot name, leaving them with a bruised heart. These wounds shape how we love, receive love, respond to conflict, protect ourselves, and repeat patterns we don't fully understand when triggered. Modern relationships are more emotionally complex than ever, not because people have changed, but because we now have the language to see what has always been there.

At the heart of these patterns is something I call attachment drama the emotional loops created by early relational wounds, the nervous system's fear responses, and the behaviors we learned long before adulthood. When these patterns go unrecognized, they become the quiet engines driving an emotional storm full of conflict, avoidance, anxiety, and the feeling that love is either too hard or too fragile.

The Attachment Drama Healing Method™ exists to help you see what has been shaping your emotional world often for decades.

This method combines emotional insight with clinical clarity, giving you a practical framework for understanding your attachment patterns, healing your relational wounds, and breaking the cycles that keep pulling you back into the same painful experiences time and time again.

You are not starting over.
You are simply learning what no one taught you about trauma.

What Is the Attachment Drama Healing Method™?

The Attachment Drama Healing Method™ is a structured, research-informed system designed to help you break patterns:

- Understand the emotional "story" created in your early years
- Identify how that story impacts your relationships today
- Recognize trauma-driven patterns in yourself and others you love
- Break drama cycles of emotional conflict, avoidance, and self-sabotage
- Build secure emotional habits and healthier relational boundaries

This method draws from:

- Attachment theory
- Inner child work
- Emotional trauma psychology
- Nervous system regulation

- Family systems and generational patterns
- Real-life behavioral observation
- Clinical emotional development

The specifics differed.

The emotional patterns did not.
People struggled with:

- Feeling unseen or misunderstood
- Avoidance that protected them but destroyed connection
- Anxiety that made closeness feel unsafe
- Fearful-avoidant cycling

But unlike purely academic approaches, this method also honors the emotional reality the lived experience of the human heart.

It merges clinical understanding with compassion, narrative, and intuitive reflection, allowing you to engage not just with your mind, but with your emotional truth.

The Attachment Drama Healing Method™ is an original, proprietary emotional wellness system created and developed by **Johanna Sparrow (Antoinette M. Watkins)** under **Blue Shoes Publishing**. This method serves as the foundation of my entire literary and educational body of work, including my flagship novel series *Fearful Meets Dismissive, Anxious Meets Fearful,* and future titles within **The Attachment Drama Healing Series™.**

Each book and workbook within this collection is rooted in the concepts, principles, and practices introduced here. All titles, themes, characters, and symbol systems appearing within this method and its related creative works are the intellectual property of the author and are protected under U.S. copyright and trademark law. No portion of this method or its associated works may be reproduced, adapted, or used in any form without written permission from the author or Blue Shoes Publishing.

The specifics differed.

The emotional patterns did not.
People struggled with:

- Feeling unseen or misunderstood
- Avoidance that protected them but destroyed connection
- Anxiety that made closeness feel unsafe
- Fearful-avoidant cycling

- Emotional shutdown
- Over-functioning in relationships
- Choosing partners who recreated childhood pain
- Losing themselves in the hope of being loved

These behaviors weren't random.
They were patterned from the start.
They were survival strategies.
They were the emotional handwriting of early-life experiences.

The Attachment Drama Healing Method™ emerged from my desire to create a system that explained why these patterns exist and how to change them with clarity, compassion, and practical steps.

The Emotional Crisis of Modern Relationships

Today's relationships carry layers of complexity that previous generations never addressed:

- People are overwhelmed, overstimulated, and emotionally under-supported.
- Childhood trauma is now widely recognized but rarely understood.
- Fear of intimacy and longing for connection coexist in the same person.
- Technology allows constant contact but not genuine closeness.
- Many adults never learned emotional regulation, communication, or secure attachment.

As a result:

- Avoidant partners shut down.
- Anxious partners overreach.
- Fearful-avoidant individuals cycle between longing and withdrawal.
- People bond quickly but cannot maintain emotional safety.
- Conflict becomes the battleground for unhealed wounds.
- Love feels like instability instead of comfort.

This book was created to help you understand the emotional crisis within yourself and the emotional crisis happening in the people you love.

How Attachment Drama Shapes the Human Life Cycle
Attachment drama doesn't begin in adulthood.
 It begins in:

A person's childhood

When safety is inconsistent or unavailable, the child learns to adapt emotionally in ways that feel normal but later become harmful to people they claim to love.

Adolescence

Early wounds begin shaping identity, self-worth, and the types of connections and love teens seek.

Adulthood

Old emotional scripts repeat in your daily life as:

- Relationship sabotage
- Emotional withdrawal
- Overattachment and anxious pursuit
- Fear of abandonment
- Attraction to emotionally unavailable partners
- Difficulty trusting closeness
- Reactivity during conflict

Attachment drama follows a person across their entire life—until they become aware of the pattern and choose to interrupt it once and for all.

And this book teaches you how to interrupt attachment drama.

How to Use This Book
This book is designed as a guided emotional and psychological experience, not just information, but a clear path to happiness. Each chapter includes:
- Clinical explanations of emotional patterns
- Real-world examples of attachment in action
- Reflection prompts for self-awareness
- Integration exercises for healing
- Narrative-style explanations to support emotional processing

You can use this book:

- For self-healing

- As part of a relationship or emotional work
- As a companion to therapy
- As preparation for the upcoming series titles
- As a tool for generational healing within your family

There is no right or wrong way—only your way.
Go at your own pace.
Take breaks when needed.
Return to sections that stir emotion.
Healing is not linear, but it is possible.

About the Companion Titles

This Foundation Book is the beginning of a larger emotional ecosystem from Johanna Sparrow.

The next major title in the Attachment Drama Healing Series™ is:

Fearful Meets Dismissive
- Adult Edition
- Teen Edition
- Pre-Teen Edition

Each version teaches emotional awareness and attachment healing appropriate for its age group.

More titles will follow in Johanna Sparrow's signature emotional-clinical style, continuing the mission of helping readers understand themselves, their partners, and their emotional world more deeply.

CHAPTER 1
THE BIRTH OF ATTACHMENT DRAMA

Every emotional story begins long before adulthood.

Long before we fall in love for the first time, long before heartbreak or the fear of abandonment take shape, our attachment story is quietly forming inside us. It forms in the early, impressionable spaces of childhood where safety is either available or unpredictable, where trust is built or broken, love is given or taken, and where love is either nurturing or confusing.

In those first tender moments of life, the emotional blueprint that shapes every future relationship begins to write itself regardless of our awareness.

Most people never realize that the way they love, argue, cope, or emotionally retreat as adults is deeply rooted in the earliest experiences they had with their caregivers. Whether love felt warm and predictable or inconsistent and emotionally dangerous, your body learned how to respond, adapt, and survive. These adaptations became your attachment style your internal map of what connection means whether positive or negative.

How you hold, chase, fear, sabotage, or avoid love in adulthood is not random.

It is the result of the emotional patterns your nervous system learned before you ever had words to explain them.

Attachment drama arises when those early emotional imprints collide with adult experiences of intimacy, conflict, and vulnerability, sparking chaos and deep-rooted confusion. There is an internal tug-of-war between the child in you, who once needed to feel safe, and the adult in you, who seeks connection, love, and acceptance. It is where the past and present blur, creating reactions that feel overwhelming, confusing, or out of proportion, leaving you a broken version of your true self.

To understand your relationships, you must understand where the story began.

⍦ Early Childhood Imprints

Attachment will always begin with a single question:
Was someone there for me when I needed them?

If, as a child, you experienced consistent warmth, affection, and responsiveness, your nervous system learned:

"I am safe. I am loved. I am protected, and my needs matter."

This imprint sets the foundation for secure attachment an internal belief that relationships can be stable, supportive, and emotionally safe.

But if early experiences were marked by:

- unpredictability
- criticism
- emotional distance
- chaos or conflict
- fear of upsetting a caregiver
- being ignored or dismissed
- being shamed for expressing needs
- inconsistent affection
- physical absence or emotional withdrawal

Your nervous system learned something very different, that the world is hostile and everyone in it.

A child will never interpret behavior.
A child will most always internalize it.

A child who experiences inconsistent love will always believe:

- "Something is wrong with me."
- "I have to earn love."
- "My feelings drive people away."
- "I'm too much."
- "I'm not important."
- "People leave."
- "It's safer not to feel."

These early interpretations eventually become adult behaviors:

- choosing emotionally unavailable partners
- over-giving to feel worthy
- avoiding closeness
- shutting down during conflict
- clinging to relationships out of fear
- confusing chaos with passion
- mistaking anxiety for love

Early childhood imprints rarely stay in childhood.
They follow us quietly, sharply, faithfully throughout life.

Emotional Wounds & Hidden Scripts

When a child experiences emotional injury, the heart creates a script an unconscious expectation of how relationships will unfold. These scripts shape how you show up in love; even if you're unaware of them, they control your responses, actions, and behaviors.

For example:

- A child ignored when upset may grow into an adult who suppresses emotions.
- A child criticized harshly may become an adult with deep self-doubt.
- A child who learned love is conditional may overextend themselves to maintain connection.
- A child with unpredictable caregivers may develop anxiety in relationships.

- A child raised around emotional shutdown may learn to
  avoid closeness.

These scripts live beneath awareness.
We do not choose them; we repeat them.

Not because they are healthy—
but because they are familiar.

And the familiar feels safe, even when it hurts.

Generational Patterns

Attachment drama is not created in isolation.
It is passed down through generations.

The way your caregivers loved was shaped by *how they were loved.*
Their wounds became your blueprint.
Their coping behaviors became your survival strategy.
Their emotional limitations became your emotional landscape.

We inherit:

- fear of abandonment
- emotional avoidance
- conflict patterns
- communication habits
- love philosophies
- expectations of closeness
- attachment insecurities

You are not repeating your parents' life cycle.
You are repeating what your nervous system learned was "normal."

Healing these patterns is not about blame; it is about awareness.

To heal, you must recognize the emotional inheritance you never asked for.

The Birth of Attachment Drama

Attachment drama begins the moment:

- A childhood wound is triggered in adulthood
- An old emotional script tries to replay out in your life
- A partner's behavior activates a deep fear
- A moment of vulnerability mirrors a past injury
- The nervous system reacts faster than logic

This is why relationships can feel:

- intense
- overwhelming
- frightening
- addictive
- confusing
- unpredictable

This is why small arguments feel like abandonment.

Why silence feels like punishment.
Why closeness feels threatening.
Why love feels unsafe.

The person you love becomes the person you fear hurting you not because of who they are, but because the past taught your nervous system to see love as pain.

Healing begins when you identify these moments and understand why they carry so much emotional power in your life.

Reflection & Integration

Look for the Attachment Drama Healing Method™ symbols to guide your emotional insights.

1. How did your caregivers respond to your emotions?
2. (Warm? Distant? Consistent? Unpredictable?)
3. As a child, what did you learn about love?
4. (Love must be earned? Love is safe? Love is unstable?)
5. What emotional patterns do you see repeating in your adult relationships?
6. When you feel triggered or overwhelmed, what childhood feeling does it resemble?
7. What behaviors in others activate your deepest fears?

This is the first step in breaking the cycle.

CHAPTER 2
THE FOUR ATTACHMENT STYLES & THEIR DARK SIDES

Attachment shapes how we love, connect, argue, apologize, distance, and return. It influences how we handle emotional threat, what we fear in relationships, and how deeply we allow ourselves to be known, or how we disconnect to protect ourselves.

While many people understand the basic definitions of attachment styles, far fewer understand the emotional undercurrents the hidden drivers that surface under stress, fear, or emotional activation, leading to confusion and chaos.

To heal, you must understand the emotional architecture of your attachment style.
This chapter breaks down each style with compassion, not judgment.

Remember: attachment styles are survival strategies, not character flaws. When you look deeply you will see it.

♡ Secure Attachment

"I am safe. I am worthy. Love is available."

Securely attached individuals grew up with caregivers who were consistent, responsive, and emotionally attuned to their needs. And where they learned that emotional expression is safe and that closeness is comforting, not threatening.

Healthy Traits

- Comfortable with intimacy
- Honest communication
- Emotionally balanced
- Trusting and trustworthy
- Willing to repair conflict
- Able to soothe themselves and others
- Does not fear abandonment or engulfment

The Dark Side

Even secure individuals experience emotional injury.

Under stress, they may:

- Take responsibility for other people's emotions
- Over-function to "keep the peace"
- Try to "fix" or rescue their partner
- Become anchors for partners who destabilize easily
- Experience burnout in unbalanced relationships

Security is not perfection it is emotional resilience. It means repair is possible, vulnerability is survivable, and healing is available.

△ **Anxious Attachment**

"Please don't leave me."

An anxiously styled attached individual often grew up with caregivers who were warm and loving one moment and distant the next. Love felt unpredictable and confusing. Emotional attunement was not guaranteed, leaving behind a broken child.

The child learned:

"I must chase connection. I must earn love."

Healthy Traits

When balanced, an anxious attacher are likely to:

- Be deeply empathetic
- Be emotionally expressive
- Loyal and committed
- Be intuitive to others' feelings
- Be affectionate and passionate
- Capable of meaningful emotional depth

The Dark Side

Under emotional threat, they may:

- Feel abandonment intensely
- Overanalyze tone, distance, or silence
- Interpret neutral behavior as rejection

- Over-communicate during conflict
- Seek reassurance repeatedly
- Confuse intensity with intimacy
- Lose their sense of self in relationships

Anxious attachers do not want too much love, they want consistent love.

Anxious attachers do not fear love.
Their fear is the loss of it.

⊗ Avoidant Attachment

"I feel safer alone."

Avoidantly attached individuals often had caregivers who were emotionally distant, overwhelmed, dismissive, or expected emotional independence far too early.

The child learned:

"It's safer not to rely on anyone."

Healthy Traits

When grounded, avoidants are:

- Independent and self-sufficient
- Calm under pressure
- Logical and steady
- Protective and loyal

- Good providers
- Less reactive in high-stress moments

The Dark Side

Under emotional stress, an avoidant may do the following:

- Shut down emotionally
- Withdraw during conflict
- Minimize the importance of feelings
- Become dismissive or distant
- Feel suffocated by closeness
- Fear losing autonomy more than losing the relationship

Their biggest fear is not abandonment, but emotional engulfment.

They disconnect to feel safe and protect their peace.

Avoidants are often mislabeled as cold or uncaring, but in truth, they are protecting the most fragile, vulnerable parts of themselves.

▽ Fearful-Avoidant (Disorganized) Attachment

I want you close but I don't trust closeness."

Fearful-avoidant individuals experienced a confusing mixture of closeness and danger in childhood. Their caregivers may have been:

- frightening
- unpredictable
- emotionally unstable
- abusive
- neglectful
- the same source of both comfort and pain

The child learned:

"The person I need is also the person who hurts me."

Healthy Traits

When healing, fearful-avoidants are:

- Deeply insightful and empathetic
- Emotionally perceptive
- Capable of intense, meaningful connection
- Highly self-aware
- Strong in emotional transformation

Looking into the Dark Side

Under threat or vulnerability, the fearful-avoidant may:

- Crave closeness while simultaneously fearing it
- Pull partners close, then push them away
- Experience emotional flooding
- React sharply to perceived rejection
- Feel unsafe depending on anyone
- Swing between anxious and avoidant behaviors

Fearful-avoidants live in an internal tug-of-war:

"Come closer... no, go away."

They desire intimacy, but fear betrayal.
Their nervous system is wired for both longing and protection,
yet neither can coexist in the same space.

Trauma Pairing Dynamics

Certain attachment styles are drawn to each other, not because
It is healthy, but it mirrors their childhood emotional
dynamics.

Below are the most common and most painful trauma
pairings:

△ Anxious + Avoidant

The most common pairing.
 One pursues, the other withdraws.
 The anxious partner feels rejected; the avoidant partner feels
overwhelmed.
 Both are reenacting childhood patterns.

▽ Fearful-Avoidant + Anyone

Creates cycles of chaos, closeness, passion, and pain.
Their internal conflict becomes the relationship's emotional
climate.

Secure + Insecure ▽ ♡

One stabilizes, the other destabilizes unless healing occurs. This can be transformative, or draining leaving behind a cycle of trauma.

♡ Secure + Secure

The least dramatic pairing but the most stable, safe, and nurturing. Understanding your attachment style helps you choose not what feels familiar, but what feels healthy.

Reflection & Integration

Look for the Attachment Drama Healing Method™ symbols to guide your emotional insights.

Take a moment to explore:

1. Which attachment style do you identify with the most? Why?
2. What behaviors in yourself do you now see as survival rather than character flaws?
3. Which attachment styles have you been most drawn to in relationships?
4. Do you notice repeating patterns in who you choose and who you avoid?
5. What part of intimacy feels safest to you? What feels most threatening?

Your attachment style is not your destiny.
It is your starting point to healing.

CHAPTER 3
THE DRAMA CYCLE

Trigger ›› Reaction ›› Collapse ›› Reconnection
Every relationship healthy or hurting—moves through emotional cycles and drama filled chaos.
But when two people carry unhealed attachment wounds, the cycle becomes louder, faster, and far more destabilizing. What begins as a minor misunderstanding spirals into emotional injury, miscommunication, fights and self-protection.

This repeating loop is what I call The Drama Cycle™, a core pillar of the Attachment Drama Healing Method™.
It reveals:
- Why relationships feel unstable
- Why communication breaks down
- Why the same argument returns again and again
- and why love can feel unsafe even when it's real

The Drama Cycle™ isn't about blaming yourself or your partner.
It's about understanding the emotional engine beneath your reactions.

Once you see the cycle, you can stop participating in it.

The Five-Stage Drama Cycle™

Every insecure attachment pattern anxious, avoidant, fearful-avoidant moves through the same emotional sequence. Even if you don't notice it consciously, your nervous system does.

It senses every shift, every micro-expression, every pause, every tone change in your frequency.

Let's break down each stage.

Stage 1: TRIGGER
A moment when an old emotional wound is activated in your life.

Triggers are rarely about what's happening now.
They are about the emotional memories stored in the nervous system long ago.

A trigger can be something small:

- a slow reply
- a change in tone
- a distracted partner
- lack of affection

Or something larger:

- betrayal
- abandonment threats
- emotional distance
- escalating arguments
- emotional unsafety

Triggers have power because they come from the past.
You are not reacting to the person in front of you.
You are reacting to the feeling inside you that was never addressed.

The child in you rises first.
Your nervous system says:
- "This feels familiar."
- "This feels unsafe."
- "This feels like before."

And in that split second, you shift into survival mode mode to protect yourself from drama.

Stage 2: REACTION

The emotional response is rooted deep in your attachment style, and each attachment style responds differently to emotional threat.

Anxious Attachment Reaction
- seeks instantly to reconnect
- texts repeatedly
- overexplains
- panics internally
- interprets silence as abandonment
- becomes hyper-aware of emotional shifts

For the anxious attachment style:

Distance = danger.

 Silence = rejection.

 Slowness = abandonment.

Avoidant Attachment Reaction
- shuts down
- detaches emotionally
- avoids communication
- minimizes the issue
- becomes distant or cold
- needs space to feel safe

Avoidants retreat not to punish, but to prevent being overwhelmed.

Fearful-Avoidant (Disorganized) Reaction

- craves closeness but fears it
- pushes their partner away, then pulls them back
- reacts intensely
- becomes overwhelmed quickly
- fears betrayal and abandonment simultaneously

Fearful-avoidants communicate from emotional turbulence, not malice.

Secure Attachment Reaction

- communicates clearly
- seeks resolution
- stays grounded
- attempts emotional repair

Even secure partners can become destabilized in chaotic, insecure dynamics.

Stage 3: COLLAPSE

The emotional breaking point

Collapse is the moment the body says:

"I am overwhelmed."

Collapse can look like:

- withdrawal
- emotional numbness
- explosive arguments
- shutting down
- crying
- stonewalling
- leaving the room
- blocking communication
- spiraling anxiety

- apologizing excessively
- giving up

Collapse is painful, but not failure.

It's the emotional point where the nervous system reaches capacity for the emotional drama.

For fearful-avoidants, collapse can be both shutting down *and* falling apart.

This is the heart of Attachment Drama.

Stage 4: RECONNECTION

The emotional reset that calms the storm

Reconnection can be:

- Through physical ("hug, touch, intimacy")
- emotional ("I'm sorry," "I miss you")
- relational (coming home, reopening communication)
- avoidance-based ("let's pretend nothing happened")

Reconnection temporarily resets the nervous system.

It brings relief.

But here's the truth:

Reconnection does NOT equal repair and never will.

This is where couples get trapped.

They reconnect, but they don't heal.

Why The Drama Cycle Feels Addictive

These cycles create emotional highs and lows:

- anxiety
- fear
- relief
- closeness

- disconnection
- longing
- unpredictability

The nervous system becomes addicted to the up-and-down drama. Love begins to feel like survival rather than safety. Breaking this cycle is not about willpower. It's about awareness, regulation, and healing the root wound deep within.

This book teaches you how.

How to Break the Drama Cycle™

Awareness is the first step, but not the last.
Healing requires:

✓ Naming the trigger
✓ Understanding the wound underneath it
✓ Regulating your emotional response
✓ Communicating from grounded presence
✓ Choosing repair instead of recycling
✓ Building secure behaviors

When you interrupt even one stage, you change the entire pattern. Eventually, the cycle stops controlling your relationship and everyone around you.

Reflection & Integration

Look for the Attachment Drama Healing Method™ symbols to guide your emotional insights.

Take a moment to reflect on your own Drama Cycle™:

1. Which stage do you get stuck in the most—trigger, reaction, collapse, or reconnection?
2. What are the most common triggers in your relationships?
3. How does your nervous system react when you feel unsafe?

1. What does "collapse" look like for you personally?
2. Do you use reconnection as repair or as avoidance?

Awareness is the first step in breaking the emotional loop.
But healing comes from understanding the deeper story beneath the pattern hiding within.

The Johanna Sparrow Method™

Where therapeutic insight meets emotionally grounded storytelling

Facts educate the mind for a life time.
Stories reach the heart forever.

This method blends both.

The Johanna Sparrow Method™ transforms every story into:

- a mirror
- a lesson
- a therapeutic companion

Readers don't just "learn" about patterns they *see themselves in* them.

This foundation prepares the heart for what comes next in your series, especially:

- Fearful Meets Dismissive™ (Adult Edition)
- Fearful Meets Dismissive™ (Teen Edition)
- Fearful Meets Dismissive™ (Pre-Teen Edition)

...with many more titles coming soon in the Johanna Sparrow signature style.

Your method is not simply read.
It is *experienced.*
And that experience is what heals.

CHAPTER 4
EMOTIONAL TRAUMA IN RELATIONSHIPS

Breakups • Divorce • Betrayal • Loss • Abuse • Neglect • Abandonment

Every relationship carries a history yours, theirs, and the emotional echoes both of you have taken long before ever meeting. Trauma does not begin in adulthood. It simply reveals itself to you there. Love has a way of pulling old injuries to the surface, and suddenly the things you thought you healed or learned to silence become loud, present, and overwhelming in your life.

Relationship trauma is not always dramatic. Sometimes it's quiet: emotional shutdowns, guilt, ghosting, rigid self-protection, or the soft "I'm fine" spoken through a breaking heart. Other times, it explodes through conflict, abandonment, betrayal, or fear. But whether subtle or catastrophic, trauma touches identity and reshapes how we give and receive love.

This chapter explores the emotional injuries most people quietly carry the wounds that trigger attachment drama, derail relationships, and make healing feel impossible.

To break the cycle, you must understand the emotional power these wounds hold.

Breakups: When the Heart Remembers Every Wound

A breakup is not just the end of a relationship.
It is the activation of every abandonment wound that came before it, breaking you into pieces.

Breakups are catastrophic because:

- they reopen old emotional injuries
- the nervous system interprets separation as danger
- attachment systems go into panic
- the mind replays every past loss
- your identity feels shaken

For anxious attachment styles:

A breakup feels like emotional freefall.

For avoidant attachment styles:
It feels like a collapse with no map for processing feelings.

For fearful-avoidants:

It is both relieving and devastating at the same time.

Breakups are not evidence of failure.
They reveal where healing is needed.

Divorce: When a Life Structure Collapses

Divorce is not just an ending.
It is a dismantling. a final goodbye.

You are not only grieving your partner but the life you will never have.
You are grieving:

- the version of yourself you were with them
- the future you imagined
- the foundation you built
- the stability you depended on
- the rhythm of a life once shared

Divorce trauma includes:

- emotional confusion
- fear of starting over
- attachment abandonment
- guilt
- anger
- relief (a feeling many hide in shame)
- identity disruption

Divorce trauma is real for many people.
But so is the rebirth that follows.

Betrayal: The Wound That Cuts Into Identity

Betrayal is not just about what happened.
It is about what it woke within in.

When someone you trust becomes the source of your pain, the heart breaks in layers:
- trust fractures
- identity shakes
- self-worth collapses

- security shatters

Betrayal trauma leads to:
- hypervigilance
- rumination
- anxiety
- emotional numbness
- grief–anger cycling
- fear of future intimacy

The question after betrayal is rarely:
"Why did they do this?"
It is:
"Why wasn't I enough for them to stay loyal?"
But betrayal is never proof of your inadequacy.
It is evidence of their deep emotional wounds, not yours.

Loss & Grief: When Love Has Nowhere to Go

Grief does not only come from death.
You can grieve:

- someone who walked away
- someone who is alive but emotionally gone
- a version of yourself that no longer exists
- the childhood you never had
- the partner you wished someone could become
- a relationship that never reached its potential

Grief sits in the body as many things:

- heaviness

- numbness
- quiet longing
- emotional collapse
- spiritual exhaustion
- physical tension

Attachment trauma intensifies grief because you are not only grieving a person you are grieving every part of yourself that was attached to them, you will never see again.

Grief is not weakness.
It is proof that you loved with your whole self and still lost love.

Abuse: When Love and Fear Occupy the Same Space

Abuse can be:

- emotional
- verbal
- psychological
- financial
- physical
- spiritual
- sexual

But emotional and psychological abuse often goes unnoticed because the wounds are invisible.

Abuse sounds like:

- "You're too sensitive."
- "You're imagining things."
- "Only I will ever love you like this."

- "You're the problem."

It feels like:

- confusion
- fear
- exhaustion
- guilt
- self-blame
- isolation
- staying because leaving feels even more dangerous

Abuse always rewires the nervous system.
It convinces you that the pain is normal and that there is nothing you can do to change it.

Healing begins when you finally understand:
What you endured was not love it was control dressed as affection.

Neglect: The Silent Wound That Echoes for a Lifetime

Neglect is one of the most overlooked forms of trauma worldwide.
It looks and feels like:

- emotional absence
- being ignored when upset
- care given only for physical needs
- affection withheld
- being unseen or unheard
- being told to "toughen up" instead of being soothed

Neglect teaches the child:

- "My feelings don't matter."
- "I can't rely on anyone."
- "Love is inconsistent."

As an adult, neglect shows up as:

- shutting down
- avoiding intimacy
- emotional distancing
- fear of vulnerability
- craving closeness but not trusting it
- collapsing during conflict
- withdrawing to feel safe

Neglect doesn't leave bruises.
It leaves emptiness, a void in the soul.
And emptiness becomes its own emotional inheritance, gifted to you.

Abandonment Wounds: The Root of Stability Issues

Abandonment is not always physical.
It can be emotional, spiritual, or psychological.

Attachment trauma forms when:

- someone you depended on disappeared
- needs were dismissed
- affection was inconsistent
- promises were broken
- you were left to self-soothe too early
- you felt emotionally unprotected

Abandonment wounds create:

- fear of being replaced
- emotional clinginess
- deep insecurity
- jealousy
- destructive independence ("I don't need anyone")

Abandonment wounds run deep.

They profoundly shape the adult life cycle and the relationships around them.

Why Trauma Feels Repeated in Love

People often ask:

- "Why do I keep choosing the same type of partner?"
- "Why does this keep happening to me?"
- "Why do my relationships feel like déjà vu?"

The truth is simple:

Your unhealed attachment wound chooses before you can.

Your adult relationships replicate your past experiences:

- the emotional inconsistency of childhood
- the survival patterns that kept you safe
- the familiarity of old trauma
- the love you knew, not the love you needed

You are not repeating relationships.

You, my dear, are simply repeating wounds daily.

Healing ends the repetition.

Reflection & Integration

Look for the Attachment Drama Healing Method™ symbols to guide your emotional insights.

Take a moment with yourself:

1. Which of the following has shaped your relationships most
   deeply:
2. breakup, divorce, betrayal, loss, abuse, neglect, or
   abandonment?
3. What emotional habits or fears grew from that wound?
4. How do you react when you feel emotionally unsafe?
5. Which pain still feels unresolved or ignored?
6. What part of your trauma story is asking to be healed now?

You cannot heal what you refuse to acknowledge.
And you cannot move forward while carrying pain you have
never understood or unwrapped.

This chapter marks your first step toward emotional liberation.

CHAPTER 5
COMMUNICATION FROM EACH ATTACHMENT STYLE

Understanding Communication Through the Lens of Attachment & Emotional Patterns

Communication is not just words.
It is nervous-system dialogue.
It is history speaking.
It is childhood echoing through adult conflict.
It is the emotional inheritance you never asked for showing up in how you respond, retreat, react, and reconnect.

Most couples believe they're arguing about dishes, tone, time, or attention, but they are not, and far from it. Underneath the surface, something much more profound is happening:

- Your attachment style is speaking for you.
- Your past wounds are interpreting the moment.
- Your nervous system is responding before your heart can.
- Your fear patterns are shaping your words.
- And your partner is doing the same at the exact same time.

This is why communication feels hard.
Not because the relationship is broken, but because the emotional patterns beneath it are misaligned, misunderstood, or unhealed, leading to disconnection and distance.

In this chapter, you will learn:

- How each attachment style communicates
- How each style hears and mishears meaning
- What each style is really trying to say beneath their reactions
- How communication clashes happen
- How to decode the emotional language behind your partner's behavior
- How to create safety in communication
- and how to speak in a way your partner can actually receive

Let's begin.

THE EMOTIONAL FOUNDATION OF COMMUNICATION

You don't speak from the moment, you speak from the wound.

When relationships face stress, conflict, or emotional activation, your brain shifts out of conscious communication and into patterned communication the automatic style you learned in childhood that impacts your life..

This is why people say things like:

- "I don't know why I reacted like that."
- "It just came out."
- "I didn't mean it like that."
- "I felt myself shutting down."
- "I panicked."

Because communication isn't born from logic.
It is born from:

- fear
- longing
- overwhelm
- need
- insecurity
- trauma
- attachment patterns
- emotional memory

Your communication style protects you.
But your partner's communication style protects them.
This is where relational conflict begins and why there is a disconnection or breakdown in communication.

SECURE COMMUNICATION

"I can express myself because the connection feels safe."

Secure attachment communication is based on emotional stability. The nervous system does not interpret conflict as danger. Instead, it sees it as a regular part of connection.

Core communication traits

- open and honest
- expresses needs clearly
- listens without reacting defensively
- acknowledges their partner's feelings
- seeks repair, not victory
- remains grounded during conflict
- asks for clarification rather than assuming
- apologizes without shame

- comforts their partner without losing themselves

Secure attachment communicates the belief:

"We can talk about this and still be okay."

They don't avoid difficult conversations, nor do they escalate them. They work toward a resolution because they trust the strength of the relationship.

When overwhelmed, the secure attachment may:

- withdraw briefly to regulate
- try to "fix" instead of validate
- misunderstand intense emotional responses
- get frustrated by inconsistency
- feel pressured to be the emotional anchor too often

Even a secure person can feel insecure when in a relationship with someone who consistently undermines their emotional stability.
But they always return to the center to balance their peace.

ANXIOUS ATTACHMENT COMMUNICATION

"I communicate to prevent abandonment."

For the anxious attachment, communication is survival. When they feel even slightly disconnected, their nervous system interprets it as:

- danger
- rejection

- abandonment
- emotional loss

Any breakdown in communication with an anxious attachment style leaves them feeling emotionally out of balance.

Core communication traits

- reaches out quickly when worried
- seeks reassurance often ("Are we okay?")
- overexplains to maintain connection
- analyzes tone, silence, or conversational gaps
- expresses emotions intensely
- texts multiple times when feeling ignored
- responds instantly
- misreads neutral behavior as rejection
- fears upsetting or losing their partner

Anxious communication is often misunderstood as "clingy," but in truth, it says:

"Please stay close. My safety depends on your presence."

When overwhelmed, anxious attachment styles may:

- panic internally
- spiral into worst-case thinking
- apologize excessively
- become reactive or emotional
- need immediate reassurance
- struggle to wait for responses
- fear the relationship is ending

Their communication comes from fear, abandonment, and not intention.

AVOIDANT ATTACHMENT COMMUNICATION

"I communicate to protect my emotional space."

Avoidants communicate from a place of emotional self-protection because closeness can feel overwhelming, and conflict can feel suffocating.

Where anxious attachers chase connection, avoidants protect distance.

Core communication traits

- They give short, concise responses
- Have emotionally neutral delivery
- Prefers logic over emotion
- Avoids heavy conversations
- Shuts down when pressured
- Withdraws during conflict
- May appear cold or distant
- Rarely expresses emotional needs
- communicates more through action than words

Avoidant communication often sounds like:

- "It's fine."
- "I don't want to talk about it."
- "You're overthinking."

- "I need space."

But what they really mean is:

"I'm overwhelmed. I need distance to feel safe."

When overwhelmed, avoidants may:

- go silent
- walk away
- avoid eye contact
- detach emotionally
- become hyper-logical
- minimize the issue
- shut down completely

This is not meant as punishment. It's what they have done their whole lives, their very own survival strategy, formed in childhood.

FEARFUL-AVOIDANT COMMUNICATION

"I want closeness... but I don't trust it."

Fearful-avoidants (also known as disorganized attachers) have the most complex communication style because they carry the wounds of both anxious and avoidant attachment.

Core communication traits

- emotionally intense one moment, withdrawn the next
- expresses deep vulnerability followed by retreat
- reacts strongly to perceived rejection

- fears abandonment and engulfment at the same time
- tests the relationship unintentionally
- struggles to regulate emotional expression
- becomes overwhelmed easily
- may oscillate between closeness and fear

Their communication is filled with internal contradiction:

"Come closer... no, wait... I'm scared."

When overwhelmed, fearful-avoidants may:

- shut down suddenly
- lash out emotionally
- disappear temporarily
- question their partner's intentions
- spiral internally
- crave reassurance but panic when they receive it
- engage in push–pull communication

They do not react from confusion —
They respond to trauma memory.

HOW ATTACHMENT STYLES CLASH IN COMMUNICATION

Patterns that create emotional loops

When two different attachment styles communicate, the clash often follows predictable patterns and behaviors.

△ Anxious + Avoidant

The most common and most painful communication loop.

Anxious:
 "Talk to me, don't pull away."

Avoidant:
 "I need space, you're overwhelming me."

Anxious pursues »› Avoidant retreats »› Anxious escalates »›
Avoidant shuts down

Both feel misunderstood.
 Both feel unsafe.

▽ Avoidant + Fearful-Avoidant

An emotional collision of retreat and panic takes shape, where
the
Avoidant withdraws, FA senses abandonment, FA pursues,
Avoidant retreats harder.
 The Fearful Avoidant becomes more dysregulated, and the
Avoidant shuts down completely.

Fearful-Avoidant + Anxious

A storm of intensity and fear.
Anxious seeks connection while Fearful Avoidant begins to
panic
 FA withdraws »› Anxious escalates
 FA returns »› Anxious questions safety
  • Cycle repeats

Secure + Insecure

This can be stabilizing or draining.

Secure holds space ⇥ Insecure softens
But if the insecure partner stays dysregulated, the secure partner may eventually feel overwhelmed.

Secure + Secure

Open, balanced, positive, and grounded communication.

This pairing tends to model emotional safety for others.

THE HIDDEN EMOTIONAL LANGUAGE BEHIND COMMUNICATION

What each attachment style is REALLY saying beneath the words

Sometimes it sounds like:

- "You never listen."
- "You don't care."
- "You're too emotional."
- "You're distant."

But underneath, the emotional truth is:

Anxious:

"I'm scared you will leave me."

Avoidant:

"I'm scared of losing myself when I am with you."

Fearful-Avoidant:

"I want to trust you, but I am terrified to get hurt."

Secure:

"I want to understand you."

Communication becomes healing when you respond to the emotion underneath, not the words on top.

REFLECTION & INTEGRATION
Look for the Attachment Drama Healing Method™ symbols to guide your emotional insights.

1. Which communication style sounds most like you?
2. Which one sounds most like your partner?
3. How do you communicate when you feel unsafe or overwhelmed?
4. What emotional need is hidden inside your communication patterns?
5. What is one small shift you can make to communicate from healing rather than fear?

Communication is not about perfection.
It is about awareness, compassion, and repair.

CHAPTER 6
THE ATTACHMENT DRAMA HEALING METHOD™ FRAMEWORK

Five Steps to Rewriting Your Emotional Patterns and Rebuilding Secure Connection

Healing is not a mystery it is a process.
Patterns don't shift just because you understand them.
They change because you learn how to respond differently, consistently, and with compassion.

The **Attachment Drama Healing Method™** is the emotional blueprint that helps you heal from the inside out.
It is simple, structured, and designed to guide you through both your inner and relationship worlds.

Every step helps you:

·regulate your emotional system
·understand your triggers
·break the cycle of drama
·rebuild emotional safety
·move toward secure attachment

This chapter will walk you through the five steps of this method so you can begin creating real, sustainable emotional change.

STEP 1 — AWARENESS OF YOUR PATTERNS

Healing starts the moment you see your emotional patterns clearly.

Patterns include:

- How do you react when scared
- How do you communicate when triggered
- How do you withdraw or chase
- How you interpret tone or silence
- How do you protect yourself
- How do you disconnect from your needs

Awareness is not about blaming yourself —
It's about understanding yourself.

Without awareness, you repeat the same emotional script over and over again.
With awareness, you gain the power to choose something different.

STEP 2 — REGULATION OF THE NERVOUS SYSTEM

You cannot heal from a triggered state.
Your nervous system must feel safe before you can change a pattern.

Regulation helps you:

- Pause before reacting

- breathe through emotional intensity
- calm the anxious spike
- soften the avoidant shutdown
- reduce emotional flooding
- reconnect to your logical mind

Regulation tools include:

- grounding exercises
- deep breathing
- stepping away briefly
- labeling your emotion
- physical movement
- placing a hand over your heart
- slow self-talk

Regulation gives your mind the space it needs not to get stuck, but to respond rather than react.

STEP 3 — UNDERSTANDING THE WOUND BENEATH THE REACTION

Every emotional reaction is connected to a deep, older wound.

Underneath:

- anger
- anxiety
- shutdown
- defensiveness
- withdrawal
- panic

...is a story from your past.

This step helps you ask:

- "What am I really afraid of right now?"
- "Where have I felt this before?"
- "What part of me needs support?"
- "Is this reaction coming from the present or the past?"

Understanding your past wounds gives you compassion for yourself and clarity about your emotional triggers.

STEP 4 — HEALTHY COMMUNICATION & EXPRESSION

Once you understand your emotional patterns, you learn to communicate differently with the people you love.

Healthy communication includes:

- speaking calmly
- naming your feelings
- sharing your needs
- asking for clarity
- slowing the conversation
- listening without defending
- pausing to regulate
- expressing without attacking

Healthy communication shifts relationships because it shifts the emotional climate.
This step teaches you how to speak from your healed self — not your survival patterns.

STEP 5 — REBUILDING EMOTIONAL SAFETY

Emotional safety is the foundation of every healthy
relationship today.

You rebuild safety through:

·consistency
·boundaries
·accountability
·clarity
·repair
·self-respect
·emotional honesty
·showing up for yourself and others

When emotional safety is rebuilt, trust returns.
 Connection deepens and love flourishes.

Triggers soften.
Relationships begin to breathe again.

This step is where secure attachment starts to grow one
choice, one boundary, one moment of awareness at a time.

How These Five Steps Work Together

Healing is not linear you move between steps depending on
what you're facing.

For example:

- A trigger may require **Step 2 (Regulation)** first
- Then you move into **Step 3 (Understanding)**
- And finish with Step 4 **(Communication)**

Or:

·A conflict may begin with **Step 1 (Awareness)**
·And move into Step 5 **(Rebuilding Safety)**

This method adapts to your emotional needs —
because healing must be flexible, compassionate, and human.

Reflection & Integration
Look for the Attachment Drama Healing Method™ symbols to guide your emotional insights.

1. Which step in this method feels the most challenging for you right now?
2. What pattern are you ready to become more aware of?
3. What regulation tool helps you calm your emotional system the fastest?
4. What old wound shows up most in your reactions?
5. Which step will you practice this week?

Healing is a process.
This method is your guide through that process.
You are the one who transforms your emotional world.

**ATTACHMENT STYLE
SYMBOL GUIDE™**

CHAPTER 7
HEALING YOURSELF

Rebuilding Your Emotional Foundation From the Inside Out

A Core Pillar of the Johanna Sparrow Method™

Healing is not easy. There is no one way or path to healing, only to take the journey. The journey of returning to the parts of you that were ignored, silenced, or wounded through life cycles. Healing requires honesty, patience, self-awareness, and the courage to sit with emotions that have shaped you for years.

Before you can heal a relationship, you must heal the relationship you have with yourself and your past wounds.

This chapter guides you through emotional habit rewiring, personal accountability, inner child work, boundaries, nervous system recovery, and the intimate process of building emotional safety from within.

Self-healing is not selfish.
It is how you stop carrying old pain into new relationships.
It is how you stop repeating emotional patterns.

It is how you finally become the safe place you were missing.

The Truth About Self-Healing

Most people believe healing is about:

- trying harder
- being more patient
- avoiding triggers
- pleasing their partner
- ignoring their needs
- "moving on"
- "being strong"

Healing is never about perfection.
Healing is about:

- meeting the wounded parts of you with compassion
- learning how your nervous system responds to emotional pain
- understanding the fear beneath your reactions
- breaking emotional habits that no longer serve you
- becoming emotionally safe inside your own body
- rebuilding the attachment style you never received

Healing is a return to self and not to who you became to survive, but to who you were meant to be before the wound.

The Three Layers of Self-Healing

Every person who begins this work moves through these layers:

1. Awareness
Seeing your wounds clearly instead of blaming, denying, or avoiding.

2. Regulation

Calming the emotional storm within so you can respond from your grounded self, not your wounded self.

3. Rebuilding
    Practicing new emotional behaviors until they become your new default.
You cannot skip steps.
 You cannot heal in reverse.
 You cannot rebuild without first soothing the hurt parts inside you.

This is the emotional architecture of true change.

Returning to the Self Before the Wound

Every attachment wound was once a moment of:

- confusion
- fear
- emotional abandonment
- unmet need
- lack of safety
- emotional inconsistency
- or overwhelm

Your adult reactions shutting down, chasing, pleasing, withdrawing, panicking, or overexplaining are not personality flaws.
They are survival strategies built by your younger self.

Healing is the act of saying to that younger self:

"You are safe now.
 I'm here for you.
 You don't have to protect me alone anymore."

This is where emotional freedom takes off.

Step 1 — Seeing Your Patterns With Compassion

Healing yourself begins when you stop judging your emotional reactions and behaviors and start understanding them.

Ask yourself:
- What part of me is speaking right now my adult self or my wounded self?
- Which emotion do I feel underneath the reaction?
- What fear is trying to protect me?
- Where have I felt this before?
- What does this reaction need rather than what it demands?

Your emotions are not the enemy.
They are the evidence of the wound.

Step 2 — Calming the Inner Emotional World

You cannot heal from an activated state.
Your nervous system must feel safe enough to release the reaction.

Regulation tools include:

- grounding

- slow breathing
- naming the emotion
- stepping away from conflict
- soothing self-talk
- warm temperature (blanket, warm drink)
- physical movement
- journaling
- placing a hand over your heart
- asking your inner child: "What do you need right now?"

Regulation is not avoidance.
  It is how your emotional world returns to a state of safety so you can choose connection rather than protection.

Step 3 — Meeting Your Inner Child

This is the emotional core of healing yourself.
The inner child is:

- the part of you that felt unseen
- the part that never felt good enough
- the part that learned love was inconsistent
- the part who feared abandonment
- the part who thought they had to earn affection
- the part who became who others needed — not who they were

Self-healing requires re-establishing contact with that part of you and saying:

"I see you.

I hear you.

You did your best.

You deserved gentleness.
 And I will give you what you never received."
Inner child work transforms emotional survival into emotional
safety.

Step 4 — The Work of Emotional Accountability
Healing yourself means owning your patterns without shame.

Accountability sounds like:

- "I realize I shut down when I'm overwhelmed."
- "I chase because I'm afraid of losing connection."
- "I withdraw because conflict feels unsafe."
- "I over-talk because silence feels like abandonment."
- "I become defensive when I fear rejection."

This is not self-blame.
 It is emotional maturity.

Accountability gives you power.
 It turns your patterns into choices.

Step 5 — Learning to Set Boundaries With Yourself First

Most people believe boundaries are something you give others.

But true boundaries begin inside:

- I will not abandon myself to keep someone close.
- I will not silence my needs to avoid conflict.

- I will not stay where I am emotionally unsafe.
- I will not break my emotional limits to secure love.
- I will not betray myself in the name of connection.

Boundary work is identity work.
It teaches you who you are beyond your wounds.

Step 6 — Building Emotional Safety From Within

Emotional safety is not something someone else gives you.
It is something you rebuild inside yourself.

It looks like:

- trusting your emotions instead of fearing them
- soothing your distress instead of spiraling
- speaking gently to yourself
- choosing repair over reaction
- allowing yourself to rest
- being patient with your healing
- validating your triggers instead of shaming them
- believing you deserve the love you desire

Emotional safety is how insecure attachment begins to heal.

Step 7 — Allowing Yourself to Become Who You Needed

Healing yourself means becoming the secure, emotionally attuned presence you never had.

This is where your adult self takes the lead:

- "I will protect you."
- "I will listen to you."
- "I will comfort you."
- "I will choose people who do not harm you."
- "I will not abandon you again."

When you become the safe space your inner child needed, the wound finally begins to close.

Step 8 — Practicing New Emotional Behaviors

Healing is not a one-time choice.
It is a daily practice.

Every small change counts:

- pausing before reacting
- asking questions instead of assuming
- speaking your needs calmly
- stepping away to regulate
- choosing repair instead of withdrawing
- giving yourself grace
- slowing the emotional spiral
- reassuring yourself
- choosing safe connections

Your nervous system rewires through repetition, not perfection.

Step 9 — Returning to Yourself

The final stage of healing is when you stop trying to become someone else and begin returning to yourself.

Not the self shaped by trauma.
Not the self molded by survival.
Not the self you pretended to be.
But the self buried underneath the wound.
Healing is not reinvention.
 It is restoration.

Reflection & Integration

Look for the Attachment Drama Healing Method™ symbols to guide your emotional insights.

Take a moment to reflect gently:

1. Which part of your emotional world feels the most wounded right now?
2. What emotional pattern are you ready to release?
3. Which inner child need do you rarely acknowledge?
4. What emotional behavior do you want to practice more consistently?
5. What does emotional safety look like for you now?
6. How can you speak to yourself with more compassion this week?
7. Which step of your healing journey are you entering today?

Remember:
 Healing is not about becoming someone new.
 It is about returning to the self you were always meant to be.

CHAPTER 8
HEALING RELATIONSHIPS

How to Repair, Rebuild, and Restore Connection After Emotional Injury

A Core Element of the Attachment Drama Healing Method™

Healing inside a relationship is one of the most courageous emotional tasks you will ever undertake. It requires honesty, patience, vulnerability, and a willingness to see both your own wounds and the wounds of the person standing in front of you.

No relationship survives on love alone.
It survives on healing.

Because relationships are not just two people trying to get along —
 they are two nervous systems, two childhoods, two emotional histories, two attachment styles, and two sets of unspoken fears learning how to dance together.
Healing in relationships is not about perfection.
 It is about repair.
 It is about learning to love in a way that does not repeat the past.
This chapter will walk you through the core elements of relationship healing inside the Attachment Drama Healing Method™, helping you understand how to reconnect, rebuild safety, and communicate in a way that honors your emotional truth.

WHERE HEALING BEGINS

Healing begins the moment one or both partners choose awareness over avoidance.

This is not about blaming each other.
This is about acknowledging:

- how your patterns collide
- where your wounds overlap
- how your communication styles trigger each other
- how emotional injuries formed
- what each person needs to feel safe
- what needs must be rebuilt
- how trust is restored

Healing is not a single moment.
It is a series of small, committed choices.

THE FOUR PILLARS OF RELATIONAL HEALING

Every couple who chooses to heal must work through these pillars:

1. Acknowledgment Without Defensiveness

Healing begins with honesty.

This means saying:

- "I see how my actions affected you."

- "I hear your pain."
- "I understand why you felt rejected."
- "My reaction hurt you, and I'm here to understand it."

Acknowledgment is not agreement.
It is emotional validation.

2. Repair Through Vulnerability

Repairing means taking accountability for your part without collapsing into shame.

Examples of healthy repair:

- "I shut down because conflict overwhelms me. I'm working on staying present."
- "I reacted harshly because I felt scared. You didn't deserve that."
- "I was emotionally distant, and I see how it hurt you."

Repair is the opposite of excuses.
It is the willingness to be emotionally honest.

3. Rebuilding Trust Through Consistency

Trust is not rebuilt through grand gestures.
It is rebuilt through:

- consistent communication
- reliable follow-through

- emotional steadiness
- transparency
- small acts of care
- predictable behavior
- responsive presence

Trust heals through repetition, not promises.

4. Creating Emotional Safety

Emotional safety is the foundation of secure connection.

It means:

- being able to express emotions without fear
- knowing your partner won't weaponize your vulnerability
- no emotional punishment or stonewalling
- being spoken to with respect
- knowing ruptures will be repaired
- feeling seen, heard, and valued

When emotional safety is restored, the relationship begins to breathe again.

HEALING IN DATING

Dating while healing requires clarity and emotional pacing.

Healing looks like:

- communicating boundaries early
- slowing down emotional intensity

- noticing red flags with compassion, not fantasy
- not using connection to soothe loneliness
- understanding your attachment triggers
- not rescuing someone who cannot meet you emotionally
- choosing partners who are consistent, not chaotic

Dating while healing is not perfect dating.

It is conscious dating.

HEALING IN FAMILY RELATIONSHIPS

Family wounds run deep because they were formed first.

Healing within family dynamics means:

- no longer playing the emotional role assigned to you
- setting boundaries with clarity and respect
- understanding generational trauma
- limiting contact when needed
- choosing emotional health over obligation
- releasing the hope that a parent may change
- grieving the parent you needed but did not receive
- Healing in family does not always mean reconciliation.

HEALING IN FRIENDSHIPS

Friendships can trigger attachment wounds too.

Healing in friendships requires:

- addressing misunderstandings quickly

- lowering emotional expectations
- valuing reciprocity
- choosing friends who respect your boundaries
- avoiding trauma-bonded friendships
- recognizing when you're over-giving to feel valued

Friendships thrive when both people feel emotionally safe.

HEALING IN BREAKUPS

Healing after separation means:

- let yourself grieve fully
- not rushing into emotional avoidance
- understanding your attachment role in the breakup
- reclaiming your identity
- redefining your boundaries
- releasing the version of yourself tied to that relationship

Breakups do not define your worth.
They reveal where your healing is needed.

HEALING IN LONG-TERM LOVE

Long-term healing requires:

- emotional maturity
- communication growth
- willingness to revisit wounds
- secure habits developed over time

- awareness of trigger patterns
- compassion during conflict
- supportive presence

Long-term relationships require continuous emotional maintenance.

THE ROLE OF PATIENCE IN HEALING

Healing requires:

- patience with yourself
- patience with your partner
- patience with the process

Emotional patterns formed over years cannot be undone overnight.

But they can be undone.

REFLECTION & INTEGRATION

Look for the Attachment Drama Healing Method™ symbols to guide your emotional insights.

1. What relationship are you currently healing or wanting to heal?
2. Which pillar of healing (acknowledgment, repair, consistency, safety) do you struggle with most?
3. What emotional pattern from your past affects your current relationships?
4. What boundary do you need to set to support your healing?
5. What does emotional safety mean to you now?

Healing does not require perfection.

It requires presence.

It requires willingness.

It requires your honest heart.

CHAPTER 9
WHEN HEALING ISN'T ENOUGH

Recognizing Patterns That Cannot Change, Protecting Your Emotional Safety, and Rebuilding After Loss
(Johanna Sparrow C/B Hybrid Edition)

Healing transforms you but transformation doesn't guarantee that every relationship will survive the journey.
 Sometimes healing gives you clarity you were not ready to face before.
 Sometimes becoming healthier reveals the emotional limitations of a relationship you worked so hard to maintain.
And this is the most painful truth of emotional growth:
Not every relationship can be healed, even when the love is real.
 And sometimes the most compassionate act you can choose... is letting go.
This chapter will help you understand when healing leads to reconnection —
 and when healing demands release.

When Emotional Patterns Cannot Change

Some people want the relationship,
 but not the responsibility.

Some want you
but not the self-awareness required to love you well.

Healing a relationship requires two willing hearts.
But deeply rooted patterns that are dismissed, denied, or
defended cannot shift.

Signs a pattern cannot change (at least not now):

- the same arguments repeat with no resolution
- your needs are consistently dismissed
- apologies come without changed behavior
- emotional safety is never rebuilt
- manipulation replaces accountability
- communication stays hostile or nonexistent
- growth is one-sided
- defensiveness blocks every attempt at repair

When one person is doing the emotional labor for two,
love becomes exhaustion, not connection.

The Difference Between Love and Emotional Safety

Love is not enough.
It never has been.

People stay in painful relationships because:

- the love is real
- the history is long
- the bond feels familiar
- the potential looks hopeful

- the fear of leaving is overwhelming
- the connection is addictive
- the hope that "it will get better" feels impossible to let go

But love without emotional safety becomes trauma, not intimacy.

Emotional safety requires:

- trust
- accountability
- consistency
- respect
- protection
- repair
- emotional presence

When these elements are missing, love becomes unstable — even dangerous.

When Staying Becomes Self-Betrayal

There is a moment in every painful relationship when you realize staying is hurting you more than leaving would.

Self-betrayal sounds like:

- silencing your needs to keep the peace
- minimizing your hurt to avoid conflict
- accepting behavior that breaks your boundaries
- holding onto potential instead of reality
- staying to avoid being alone

- shrinking yourself to be tolerable
- loving them more than you love yourself
- tolerating emotional neglect or abuse
- losing your voice, your worth, or your identity

Self-betrayal is a wound louder than heartbreak.

Choosing yourself after years of choosing someone else
is not abandonment —
it is healing.

Acceptance: The Hardest Stage of Healing

Acceptance does not mean you approve of the pain.
It means you stop fighting the truth.

Acceptance sounds like:

- "This is not good for me anymore."
- "I can't be the only one doing the emotional work."
- "They are not ready to grow."
- "I deserve a healthy love."
- "I can't keep explaining basic respect."
- "This relationship no longer aligns with my healing."
"

Acceptance frees you from false hope.
It is the moment healing becomes honesty.

The Courage to Let Go

Letting go is not giving up.
It is honoring your emotional truth.

People think leaving is the hardest part — it isn't.
The hardest part is accepting:

- you did everything you could
- you cannot save a relationship alone
- your love is not a cure for someone else's wound
- your healing revealed incompatibilities
- staying would cost you your peace

Letting go becomes the only choice
when holding on is breaking you.

When the Relationship Can Heal — and When It Cannot

A relationship CAN heal when:

- both people take accountability
- both commit to self-awareness
- both regulate emotions
- both do core wound work
- both practice vulnerability
- both rebuild trust slowly

This requires two emotionally willing adults.

A relationship CANNOT heal when:

- one person refuses change
- accountability is one-sided
- emotional abuse is present
- trust is consistently broken
- safety is never rebuilt

- remorse never leads to action
- one person becomes "the problem"
- communication stays destructive or nonexistent

Healing cannot happen in environments
that deny emotional reality.

Grieving the Relationship You Wanted

When you let go, you're not just grieving the person —
you're grieving:

- the version of yourself you became with them
- the future you imagined
- the hope you held onto
- the promises that never came true
- the potential that felt so close
- the emotional investment you gave freely

This grief is real.
It is sacred.
It is heavy.
Let yourself feel it.
Let yourself release it.
Let yourself grow through it.
Grief is not a setback.
It's a cleansing.

Rebuilding After Loss

You cannot rush healing.

You cannot fill the empty space with someone new
and expect the pain to disappear.

You must sit with yourself long enough
to understand what your heart needs next.

Rebuilding looks like:

- reconnecting with yourself
- rediscovering your voice
- defining your new needs
- healing your wounds
- strengthening boundaries
- rebuilding self-worth
- learning who you will never tolerate again
- allowing new love in slowly

Your future relationships depend on how you rebuild after
your past ones.

Healing after loss isn't about replacing someone —
it's about replacing the emotional patterns
that allowed the pain.

You Will Love Again — Differently

When you heal, you won't:

- chase unavailability
- settle for inconsistency
- ignore your intuition

- repeat the same emotional patterns
- confuse chaos with passion
- betray yourself for connection

Healing turns you into someone who chooses:

- stability
- reciprocity
- respect
- emotional presence
- secure love

Your next love will not look like your last.
Neither will you.

Reflection & Integration

Look for the Attachment Drama Healing Method™ symbols to guide your emotional insights.

Take a moment to reflect:

1. Are you in a relationship where healing is one-sided?
2. What patterns keep repeating no matter how hard you try?
3. What would choosing yourself look like right now?
4. What are you afraid of losing if you let go?
5. What are you afraid of gaining?

(Peace? Freedom? Clarity? Power?)

Sometimes the answer you need
is the one you've been avoiding.

CHAPTER 10
BECOMING SECURE

The Path to Emotional Maturity, Inner Stability, and Healthy Connection

Becoming secure is not about becoming flawless.
It's not about avoiding triggers or never feeling insecure again.

Becoming secure means learning to navigate your emotional world with awareness, compassion, and confidence.

Secure attachment is not a personality type
it is a skillset,
a mindset,
and a way of relating to yourself and others that supports emotional safety, intimacy, and stability.

Healing doesn't erase your past.
It transforms how your past shapes your present.

This chapter guides you into the secure version of yourself — the version who communicates clearly, honors your needs, chooses healthy relationships, and trusts yourself enough to move through life without abandoning who you are.

What It Means to Become Secure

A secure person does not avoid emotions.
They understand them.

They don't suppress needs, they communicate them.
They do not collapse during conflict.
They regulate and repair.

They do not lose themselves in love.
They stay grounded and whole.

Secure attachment looks like:

- emotional balance
- self-respect
- healthy boundaries
- calm communication
- the ability to trust
- accountability
- choosing partners wisely
- staying grounded during triggers
- resolving conflict without collapsing
- connecting with vulnerability
- understanding others without absorbing their emotions

You don't become secure for others.
You become secure for yourself.

The Secure Self vs. The Injured Self

You hold two emotional identities:
1. Your Injured Self - shaped by trauma
2. Your Secure Self - shaped by healing

Your injured self fears:
- abandonment
- rejection

- loss
- closeness
- betrayal
- vulnerability
- conflict

being misunderstood

Your secure self trusts:

- emotional resilience
- self-worth
- safety in connection
- internal validation
- emotional regulation
- healthy communication
- grounded love

Healing means shifting which inner voice you follow.

The Secure Identity You're Building

Becoming secure is choosing to:

✓ Communicate Instead of React
Conflict becomes conversation, not collapse.
✓ Pause Before Responding
Triggers lose power when you slow down.
✓ Name Your Needs
You stop hoping people will guess.
✓ Set Clear Boundaries
You teach others how to treat you.

✓ Stop Chasing Unavailable Partners
Your healed heart rejects emotional starvation.
✓ Choose Consistency
You replace chaos with calm.
✓ Regulate Your Nervous System
You stay grounded even when old fears rise.
✓ Let Go Without Losing Yourself
You choose your well-being over survival patterns.
✓ Love From Wholeness Instead of Fear
Love becomes a shared experience — not a rescue mission.

Healing the Nervous System

Secure attachment lives in the nervous system, not the mind.

To become secure, your body must learn:
- safety
- emotional calm
- stability
- predictability
- groundedness

Nervous system healing tools:

- slow deep breathing
- grounding movements
- warm baths or showers
- gentle stretching
- meditation or prayer
- journaling
- affirmations
- mindful self-talk

- somatic awareness
- releasing tension through movement

The safer your body feels, the easier emotional triggers become to manage.

Choosing Secure Relationships

You cannot build a secure identity in emotionally unsafe environments.

Who you choose becomes the relationship you experience.

A secure relationship is built with someone who:

- communicates openly
- respects boundaries
- apologizes sincerely
- repairs conflict
- shows consistency
- is emotionally present
- is willing to grow
- is responsible for their own healing
- values your well-being
- does not weaponize your vulnerability

This is not the relationship you hope for someday.

This is the relationship you deserve now.

Relearning Love

Love feels different when you're secure.

Love becomes:

- peaceful
- warm
- reciprocal
- stable
- supportive
- affirming
- emotionally safe
- grounded instead of chaotic
- nourishing instead of draining

You no longer confuse:

- intensity with connection
- avoidance with independence
- inconsistency with passion

You learn that love does not need to hurt to feel real.

Generational Healing

When you become secure, you break emotional patterns carried for decades, sometimes generations.

Your healing becomes:

- a new blueprint
- a new emotional standard
- a new model for children
- a new story for future generations

You may be the first in your lineage to:

- set boundaries
- choose healthy love
- practice emotional regulation
- reject generational trauma
- speak your truth
- heal attachment wounds
- build secure relationships

This is not just personal healing.
This is generational transformation.

Your healing is the legacy.

The Future You're Creating

Being secure means stepping into a new identity:

- emotionally grounded
- confident
- self-aware
- connected
- deliberate
- loving
- whole

It means choosing people, environments, and behaviors that support your healing.

It means refusing to settle for relationships that drain your spirit or wound your heart.

It means becoming the version of you who knows:

- you are worthy
- you are lovable
- you are enough
- you deserve peace
- you deserve reciprocity
- you deserve emotional stability

Becoming secure is not the end of healing —
it is the beginning of a new life.

Reflection & Integration

Look for the Attachment Drama Healing Method™ symbols to guide your emotional insights.

1. What does the secure version of you look like?
2. What behaviors do you need to release to step into security?
3. What boundaries or practices will protect your healing?
4. What relationship patterns are you no longer willing to tolerate?
5. How will you honor the person you are becoming?

Your healing is your freedom.
Your security is your power.
Your future is yours to rewrite.

Acknowledgments

Healing is never a journey we walk alone.
Every lesson in this book was shaped by the people, stories, and emotional truths that crossed my path.

To every reader, client, and soul who trusted me with your experiences —
thank you.

 Your honesty, heartbreaks, breakthroughs, and resilience formed the heartbeat of this method. Your courage taught me what healing truly looks like in real life: imperfect, brave, and deeply human.

To the emotional healers, therapists, clinicians, spiritual teachers, and everyday helpers who continue to serve those in pain —
your work makes this world safer.
You are the quiet pillars guiding others back to themselves.

To the people who taught me about love, attachment, loss, and courage —
your lessons became the foundation of this book.
You shaped the insights, the clarity, and the compassion that now live within these pages.

To anyone who has ever felt unworthy, unseen, unheard, or unloved —
your healing matters.
You were never the problem.

You were never "too much."
And you were never beyond repair.
This book was written for you.

Thank you for allowing me to hold space for your wounds, your growth, and your return to emotional safety. It is an honor to walk beside you on this journey.

ABOUT THE AUTHOR

Johanna Sparrow

(Pen name of Antoinette Maria Watkin)

Johanna Sparrow is a relationship expert, emotional wellness guide, and the creator of the **Attachment Drama Healing Method™**, the **Attachment Drama Healing Series™**, and **Therapeutic Relationship Fiction™**. For over two decades, her work has helped individuals understand emotional wounds, generational trauma, and the hidden patterns that shape relationship cycles.

Through her bestselling books, healing methods, intuitive emotional insight, and signature storytelling style, Johanna empowers readers to break generational patterns, heal attachment wounds, and step into secure, grounded love. Her compassionate yet direct voice blends psychology, spirituality, and emotional truth creating a distinctive approach that resonates deeply with readers worldwide.

Johanna Sparrow is also the founder of **Blue Shoes Publishing**, where she continues to create transformative books and emotional wellness programs for adults, teens, and children — including the expanding universe of **Attachment Drama Healing titles** such as *Fearful Meets Dismissive* (Adult, Teen, and Pre-Teen Editions), with many more to come in her signature style of emotional clarity and relationship insight.

She believes healing is not about perfection —
it is about returning to the parts of yourself that deserve love,
safety, and peace.

Attachment Drama Healing Method™ Symbol Guide

A visual map of the attachment styles, emotional patterns, and behavioral cycles explored throughout this method.
These symbols represent the emotional dynamics behind each pattern and serve as a guide for self-awareness, healing, and secure relating.

■ Secure Attachment — The Square

Meaning: Stability • Emotional availability • Consistency
The square represents grounding, structure, and reliability. Secure individuals offer emotional steadiness, open communication, and a balanced sense of self in relationships.

▲ Avoidant Attachment — The Triangle

Meaning: Distance • Independence • Self-protection
Triangles point away, symbolizing withdrawal and emotional escape. Avoidant partners often value independence over intimacy and pull back when vulnerable.

● Anxious Attachment — The Circle

Meaning: Closeness • Pursuit • Emotional looping
Circles represent continuation and return, mirroring the anxious cycle of seeking reassurance, fearing abandonment, and longing for closeness.

◑ Fearful-Avoidant Attachment — The Split Circle

Meaning: Push–pull • Mixed signals • Trauma-driven love
 Half open, half closed, the split circle reflects the fearfully avoidant struggle: wanting love deeply while being terrified of it at the same time.

△ Commitment Phobia — The Hollow Triangle

Meaning: Present but unrooted • Avoids depth
The hollow triangle looks like the avoidant symbol but empty inside, representing connection without emotional depth or stability.

↻ Narcissistic Cycles — The Spiral

Meaning: Self-focused loops • Idealize–devalue–discard
 The spiral illustrates cycles that return to the self. These patterns often include charm, withdrawal, manipulation, and repetition.

◎ Codependency — The Linked Rings

Meaning: Enmeshment • Merged identities • Loss of self
 Linked rings symbolize emotional fusion, blurred boundaries, and over-functioning in relationships.

■ Stonewalling — The Block

Meaning: Shutdown • Emotional cutoff • Disconnection
The block represents the emotional wall built during conflict,
shutting out communication and safety.

⚡ Emotional Chaos — The Lightning Line

Meaning: Reactivity • Dysregulation • Trigger spikes
Lightning reflects emotional intensity, overwhelm, and
unpredictable reactions that disrupt connection and repair.

🌱 Healing — The Seedling

Meaning: Growth • Restoration • Becoming secure
The seedling symbolizes emotional renewal learning
regulation, boundaries, responsibility, and new relational
patterns.

⊙ inside ■ The Secure Future Self — Integrated Stability

Meaning: Centeredness • Emotional maturity • Wholeness
A circle inside a square illustrates stability supporting
openness the integrated self who connects with clarity, trust,
and peace.